# Dreams Journal

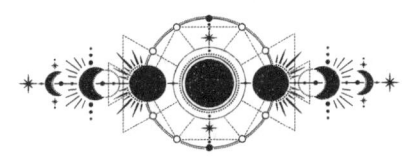

MAVEN PRESS

Copyright © Maven Press
First published in Australia in 2024
by Maven Press
Roleystone WA 6111

All rights reserved. No part of this book may be used or reproduced by any means, graphic, electronic, or mechanical, including photocopying, recording, taping or by any information storage retrieval system without the written permission of the copy-right owner except in the case of brief quotations embodied in critical articles and reviews. Because of the dynamic nature of the Internet, any web addresses or links contained in this book may have changed since publication and may no longer be valid. The views expressed in this work are solely those of the author and do not necessarily reflect the views of the publisher and the publisher hereby disclaims any responsibility for them.

 A catalogue record for this work is available from the National Library of Australia

National Library of Australia Catalogue-in-Publication

data: Dreams Journal: Maven Press

ISBN: 978-0-9756174-1-0

(Paperback)

# Dreams

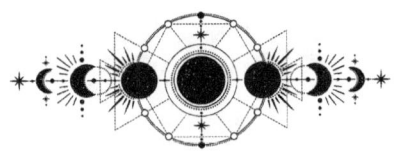

# Introduction

Welcome to the enchanting realm of dream journaling, designed to be your trusted companion on the ethereal journey through the landscapes of your dreams.

Within the pages of this dream journal, the ordinary transforms into the extraordinary, and every slumber unveils a unique adventure.

The *Dreams Journal* invites you to record the whispers of your subconscious, capturing the ephemeral beauty and enigmatic stories that unfold as you sleep.

Whether fantastical or introspective, each dream is a treasure waiting to be unveiled.

So, embark on this nocturnal journey, where the boundaries between reality and imagination blur, and the uncharted territories of your mind come to life.

May the *Dreams Journal* be the vessel that preserves the magic of your nightly wanderings, inviting you to explore the captivating tapestry of your dreamscape.

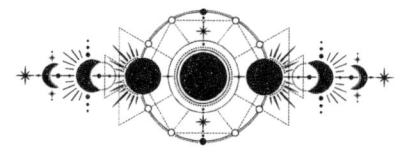

# Dreams

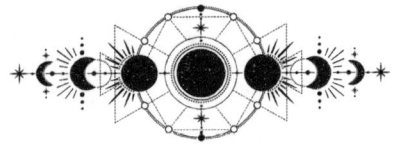

# Dreams

Date:

### How do I feel after waking?

### What was the main theme of my dream?

### Setting of dream ...

### Symbols, metaphors, people, animals and their possible meaning ...

### How does the dream relate to my life?

### Reflection

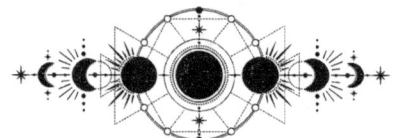

# Dreams

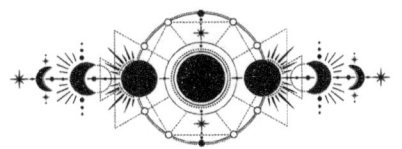

# Dreams

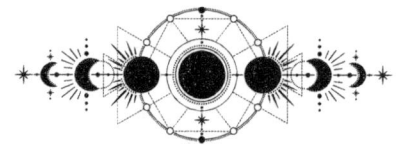

# *Dreams*

_____
_____
_____
_____
_____
_____
_____
_____
_____
_____
_____
_____
_____
_____
_____
_____
_____
_____
_____
_____
_____
_____

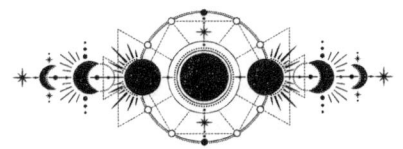

# Dreams

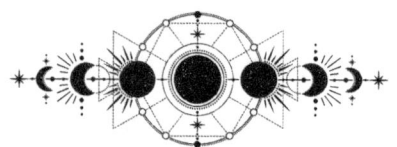

# Dreams

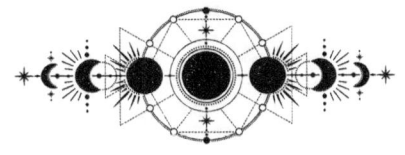

# *Dreams*

Date:

*How do I feel after waking?*

*What was the main theme of my dream?*

*Setting of dream ...*

*Symbols, metaphors, people, animals and their possible meaning ...*

*How does the dream relate to my life?*

*Reflection*

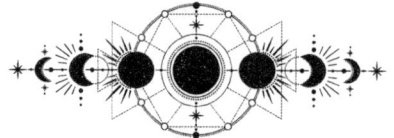

# *Dreams*

_____
_____
_____
_____
_____
_____
_____
_____
_____
_____
_____
_____
_____
_____
_____
_____
_____
_____
_____
_____
_____

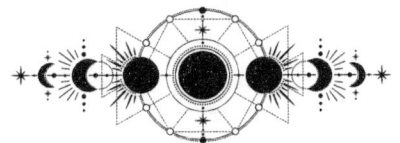

# Dreams

_____
_____
_____
_____
_____
_____
_____
_____
_____
_____
_____
_____
_____
_____
_____
_____
_____
_____
_____
_____
_____
_____
_____
_____

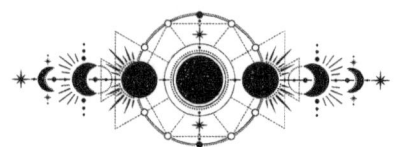

# Dreams

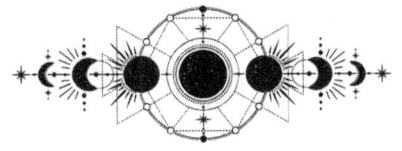

# Dreams

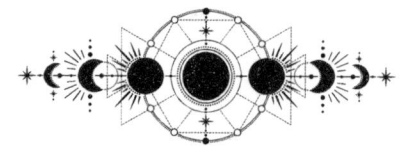

# Dreams

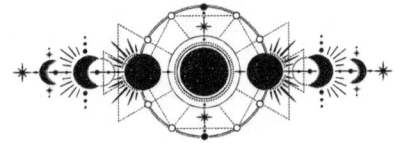

# Dreams

Date:

### How do I feel after waking?

### What was the main theme of my dream?

### Setting of dream ...

### Symbols, metaphors, people, animals and their possible meaning ...

### How does the dream relate to my life?

### Reflection

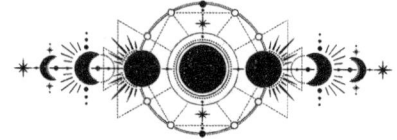

# *Dreams*

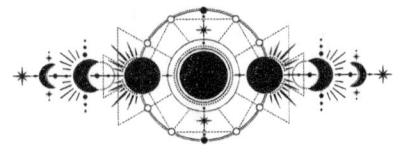

# Dreams

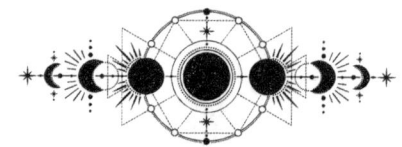

# *Dreams*

_____
_____
_____
_____
_____
_____
_____
_____
_____
_____
_____
_____
_____
_____
_____
_____
_____
_____
_____
_____
_____
_____
_____
_____

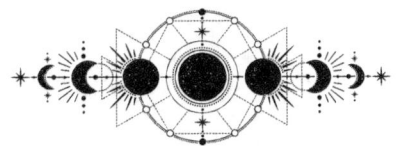

# Dreams

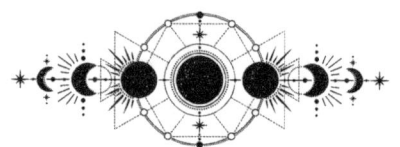

# Dreams

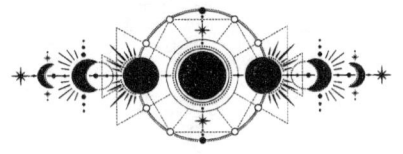

# Dreams

Date:

### How do I feel after waking?

### What was the main theme of my dream?

### Setting of dream ...

### Symbols, metaphors, people, animals and their possible meaning ...

### How does the dream relate to my life?

### Reflection

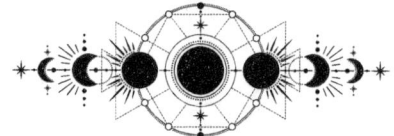

# Dreams

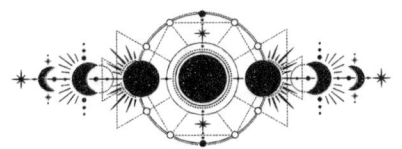

# *Dreams*

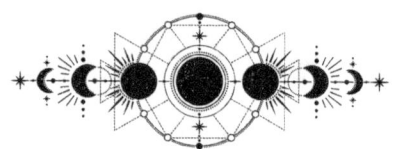

# Dreams

_____
_____
_____
_____
_____
_____
_____
_____
_____
_____
_____
_____
_____
_____
_____
_____
_____
_____
_____
_____
_____
_____

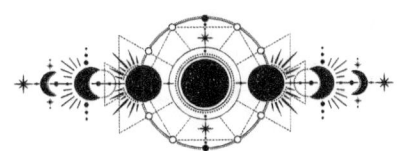

# Dreams

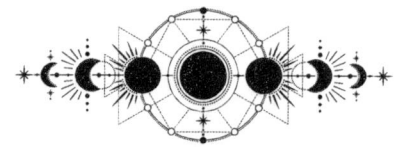

# Dreams

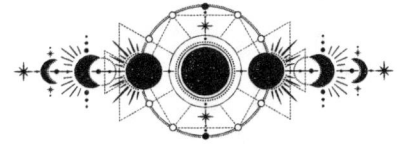

# Dreams

Date:

### How do I feel after waking?

### What was the main theme of my dream?

### Setting of dream …

### Symbols, metaphors, people, animals and their possible meaning …

### How does the dream relate to my life?

### Reflection

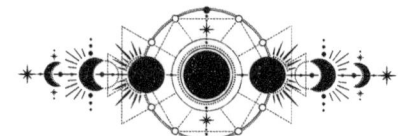

# *Dreams*

_____
_____
_____
_____
_____
_____
_____
_____
_____
_____
_____
_____
_____
_____
_____
_____
_____
_____
_____
_____
_____

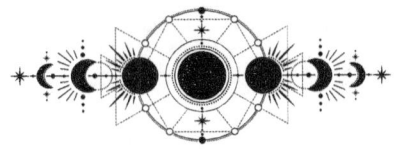

# Dreams

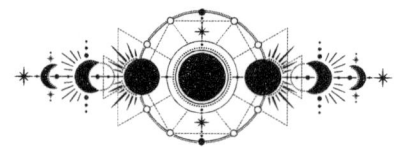

# *Dreams*

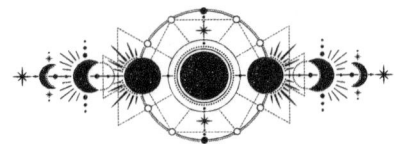

# *Dreams*

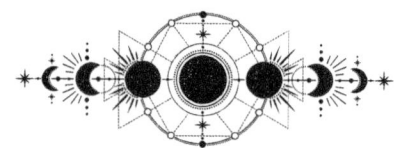

# Dreams

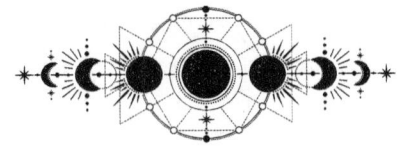

# Dreams

Date:

How do I feel after waking?

What was the main theme of my dream?

Setting of dream ...

Symbols, metaphors, people, animals and their possible meaning ...

How does the dream relate to my life?

Reflection

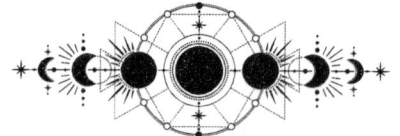

# *Dreams*

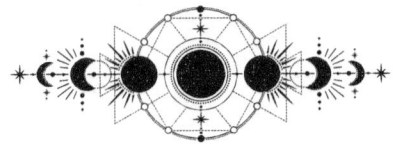

# *Dreams*

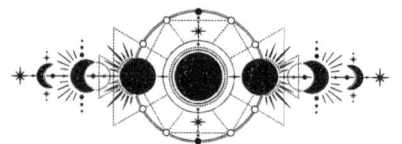

# *Dreams*

_____
_____
_____
_____
_____
_____
_____
_____
_____
_____
_____
_____
_____
_____
_____
_____
_____
_____
_____
_____
_____

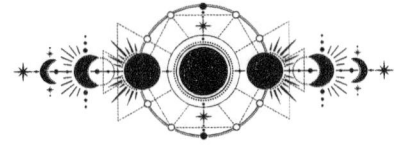

# Dreams

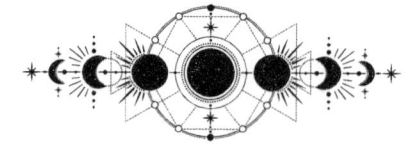

# Dreams

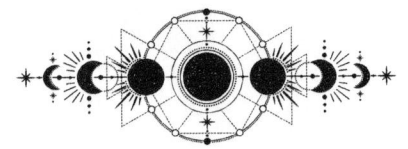

# Dreams

Date:

### How do I feel after waking?

### What was the main theme of my dream?

### Setting of dream ...

### Symbols, metaphors, people, animals and their possible meaning ...

### How does the dream relate to my life?

### Reflection

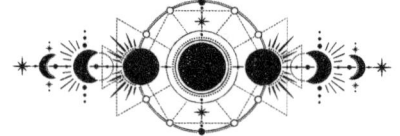

# Dreams

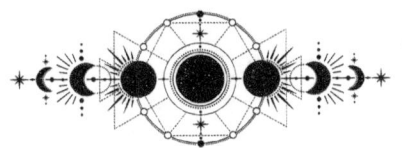

# *Dreams*

_____
_____
_____
_____
_____
_____
_____
_____
_____
_____
_____
_____
_____
_____
_____
_____
_____
_____
_____
_____
_____

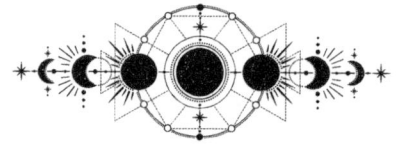

# *Dreams*

_____
_____
_____
_____
_____
_____
_____
_____
_____
_____
_____
_____
_____
_____
_____
_____
_____
_____
_____
_____
_____
_____
_____
_____

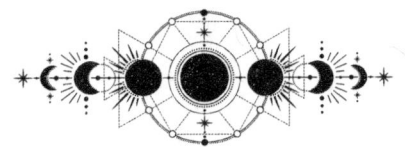

# Dreams

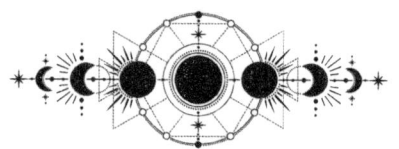

# Dreams

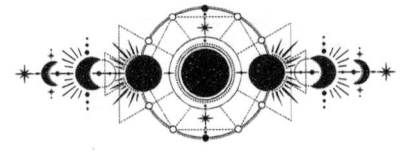

# Dreams

Date:

### How do I feel after waking?

### What was the main theme of my dream?

### Setting of dream ...

### Symbols, metaphors, people, animals and their possible meaning ...

### How does the dream relate to my life?

### Reflection

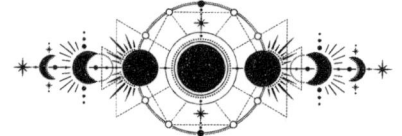

# *Dreams*

_____
_____
_____
_____
_____
_____
_____
_____
_____
_____
_____
_____
_____
_____
_____
_____
_____
_____
_____
_____
_____
_____

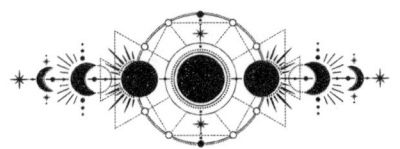

# Dreams

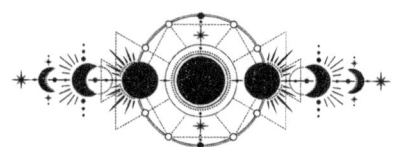

# *Dreams*

_____
_____
_____
_____
_____
_____
_____
_____
_____
_____
_____
_____
_____
_____
_____
_____
_____
_____
_____
_____
_____
_____
_____
_____
_____

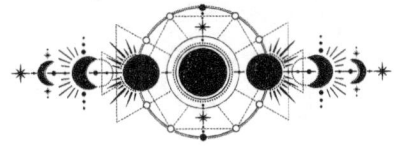

# *Dreams*

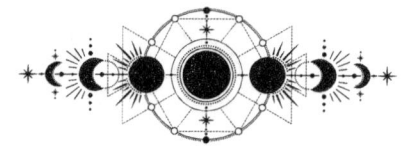

# Dreams

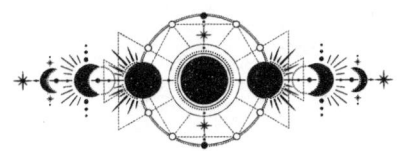

# Dreams

Date:

### How do I feel after waking?

### What was the main theme of my dream?

### Setting of dream ...

### Symbols, metaphors, people, animals and their possible meaning ...

### How does the dream relate to my life?

### Reflection

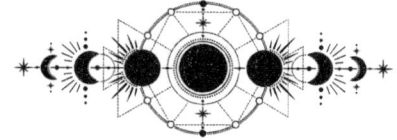

# Dreams

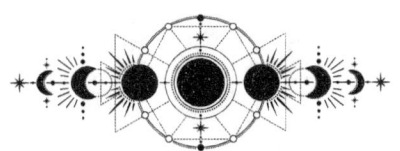

# Dreams

_____
_____
_____
_____
_____
_____
_____
_____
_____
_____
_____
_____
_____
_____
_____
_____
_____
_____
_____
_____
_____
_____
_____
_____

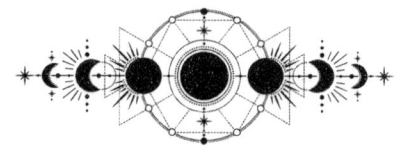

# Dreams

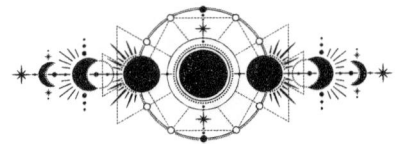

# Dreams

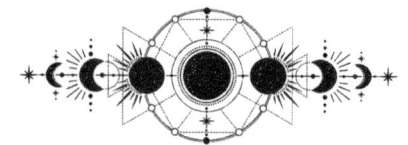

# Dreams

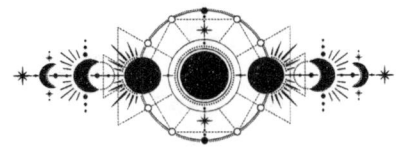

# *Dreams*

Date:

*How do I feel after waking?*

*What was the main theme of my dream?*

*Setting of dream ...*

*Symbols, metaphors, people, animals and their possible meaning ...*

*How does the dream relate to my life?*

*Reflection*

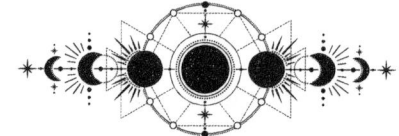

# *Dreams*

_____
_____
_____
_____
_____
_____
_____
_____
_____
_____
_____
_____
_____
_____
_____
_____
_____
_____
_____
_____
_____
_____
_____
_____
_____
_____

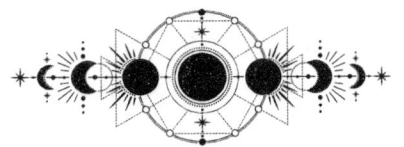

# *Dreams*

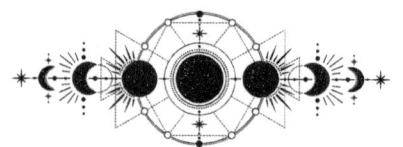

# *Dreams*

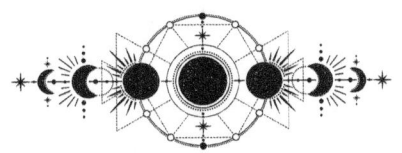

# Dreams

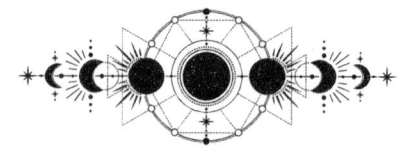

# Dreams

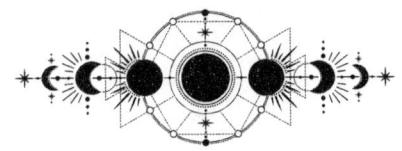

# Dreams

Date:

### How do I feel after waking?

### What was the main theme of my dream?

### Setting of dream ...

### Symbols, metaphors, people, animals and their possible meaning ...

### How does the dream relate to my life?

### Reflection

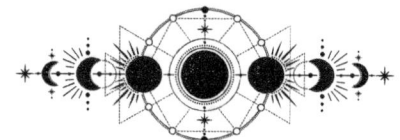

# *Dreams*

_____
_____
_____
_____
_____
_____
_____
_____
_____
_____
_____
_____
_____
_____
_____
_____
_____
_____
_____
_____
_____
_____

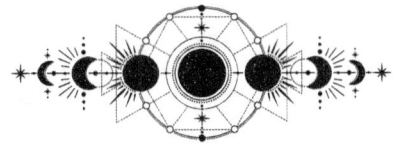

# Dreams

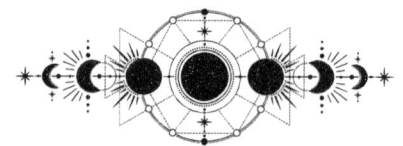

# *Dreams*

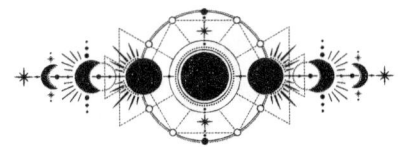

# *Dreams*

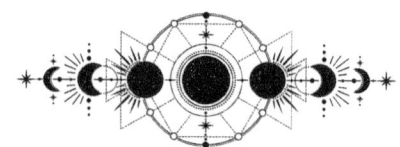

# Dreams

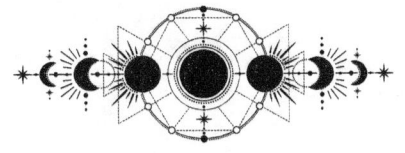

# Dreams

Date:

### How do I feel after waking?

### What was the main theme of my dream?

### Setting of dream ...

### Symbols, metaphors, people, animals and their possible meaning ...

### How does the dream relate to my life?

### Reflection

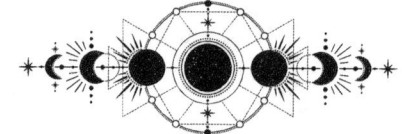

# *Dreams*

_____
_____
_____
_____
_____
_____
_____
_____
_____
_____
_____
_____
_____
_____
_____
_____
_____
_____
_____
_____
_____
_____
_____

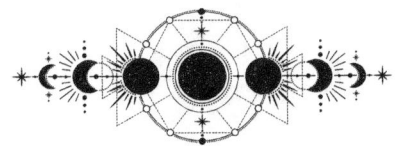

# Dreams

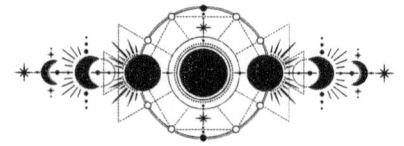

# *Dreams*

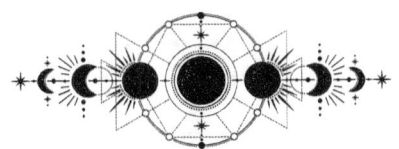

# *Dreams*

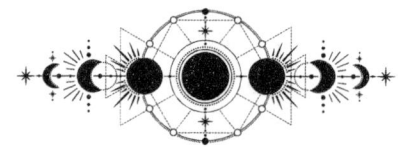

# Dreams

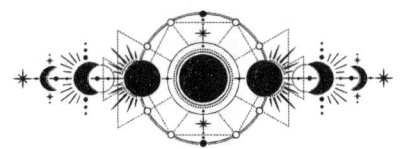

# Dreams

Date:

### How do I feel after waking?

### What was the main theme of my dream?

### Setting of dream ...

### Symbols, metaphors, people, animals and their possible meaning ...

### How does the dream relate to my life?

### Reflection

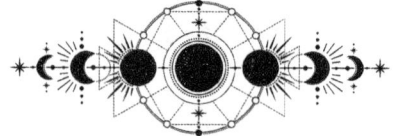

# Dreams

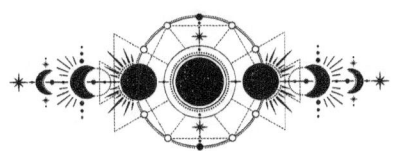

# Dreams

_____
_____
_____
_____
_____
_____
_____
_____
_____
_____
_____
_____
_____
_____
_____
_____
_____
_____
_____
_____
_____
_____
_____
_____
_____

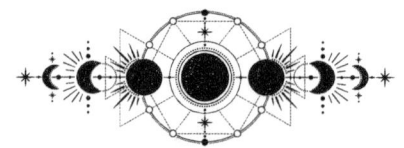

# Dreams

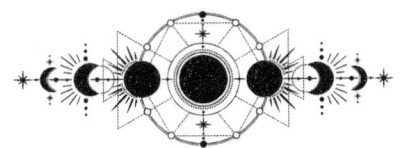

# Dreams

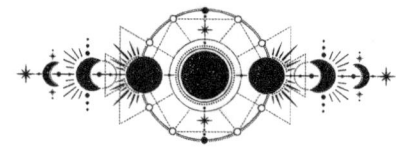

# Dreams

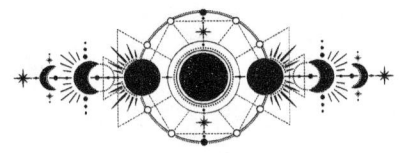

# Dreams

Date:

### How do I feel after waking?

### What was the main theme of my dream?

### Setting of dream ...

### Symbols, metaphors, people, animals and their possible meaning ...

### How does the dream relate to my life?

### Reflection

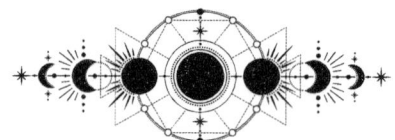

# Dreams

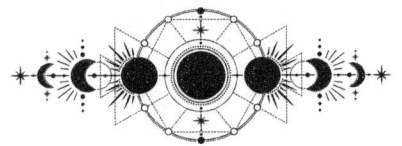

# Dreams

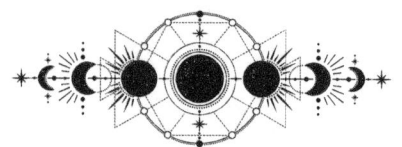

# Dreams

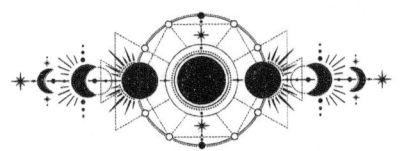

# Dreams

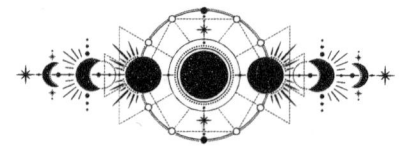

# Dreams

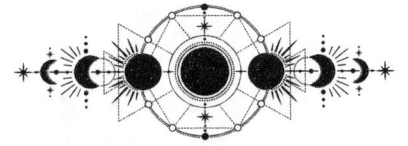

# *Dreams*

*Date:*

*How do I feel after waking?*

*What was the main theme of my dream?*

*Setting of dream ...*

*Symbols, metaphors, people, animals and their possible meaning ...*

*How does the dream relate to my life?*

*Reflection*

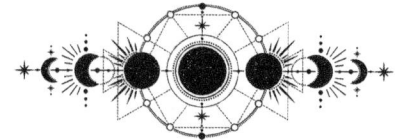

# *Dreams*

_____
_____
_____
_____
_____
_____
_____
_____
_____
_____
_____
_____
_____
_____
_____
_____
_____
_____
_____
_____
_____
_____
_____

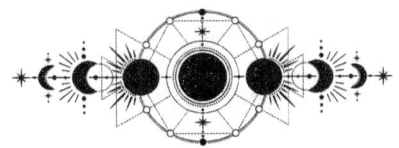

# Dreams

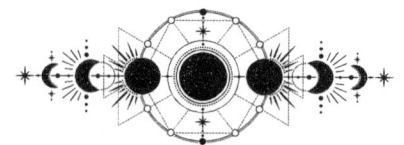

# *Dreams*

_____
_____
_____
_____
_____
_____
_____
_____
_____
_____
_____
_____
_____
_____
_____
_____
_____
_____
_____
_____
_____
_____
_____

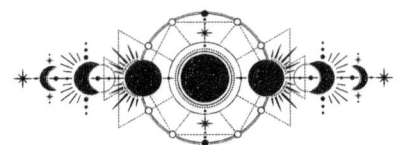

# Dreams

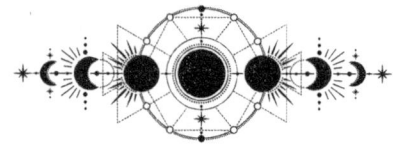

# Dreams

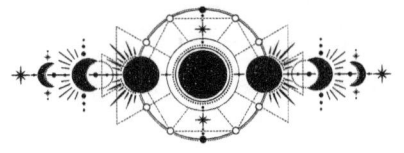

# Dreams

Date:

*How do I feel after waking?*

*What was the main theme of my dream?*

*Setting of dream ...*

*Symbols, metaphors, people, animals and their possible meaning ...*

*How does the dream relate to my life?*

*Reflection*

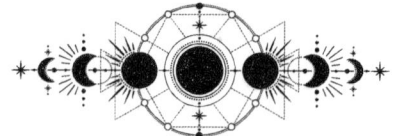

# Dreams

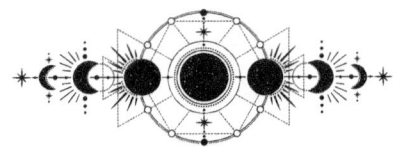

# Dreams

_____
_____
_____
_____
_____
_____
_____
_____
_____
_____
_____
_____
_____
_____
_____
_____
_____
_____
_____
_____
_____
_____
_____
_____
_____

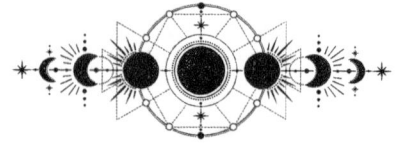

# Dreams

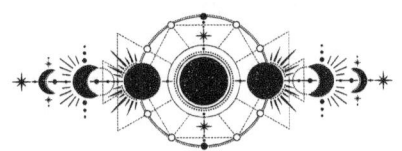

# Dreams

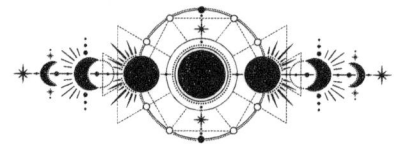

# Dreams

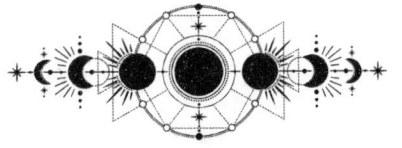

# Dreams

Date:

### How do I feel after waking?

### What was the main theme of my dream?

### Setting of dream ...

### Symbols, metaphors, people, animals and their possible meaning ...

### How does the dream relate to my life?

### Reflection

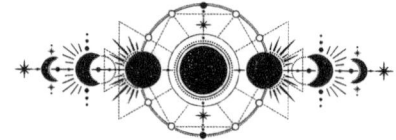

# *Dreams*

_____
_____
_____
_____
_____
_____
_____
_____
_____
_____
_____
_____
_____
_____
_____
_____
_____
_____
_____
_____
_____
_____

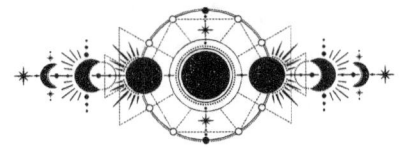

# Dreams

_____
_____
_____
_____
_____
_____
_____
_____
_____
_____
_____
_____
_____
_____
_____
_____
_____
_____
_____
_____
_____
_____
_____
_____

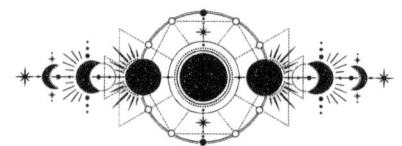

# *Dreams*

_____
_____
_____
_____
_____
_____
_____
_____
_____
_____
_____
_____
_____
_____
_____
_____
_____
_____
_____
_____
_____

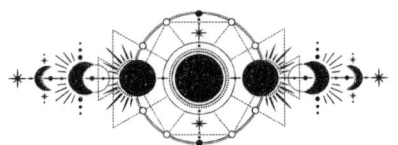

# *Dreams*

_____
_____
_____
_____
_____
_____
_____
_____
_____
_____
_____
_____
_____
_____
_____
_____
_____
_____
_____
_____
_____
_____
_____

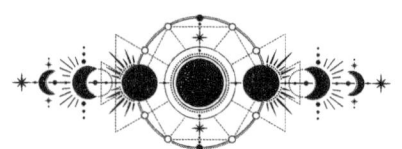

# Dreams

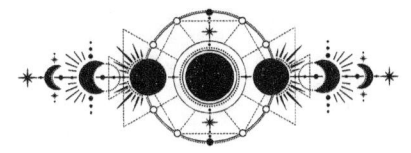

# Dreams

Date:

### How do I feel after waking?

### What was the main theme of my dream?

### Setting of dream ...

### Symbols, metaphors, people, animals and their possible meaning ...

### How does the dream relate to my life?

### Reflection

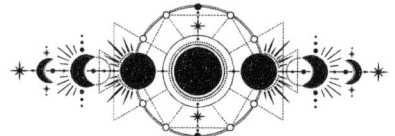

# Dreams

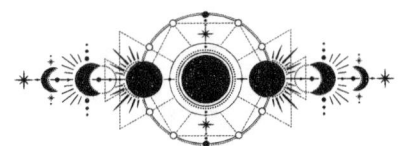

# Dreams

_____
_____
_____
_____
_____
_____
_____
_____
_____
_____
_____
_____
_____
_____
_____
_____
_____
_____
_____
_____
_____

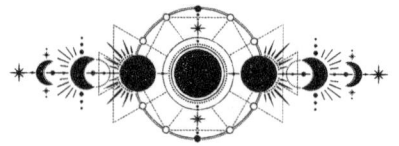

# Dreams

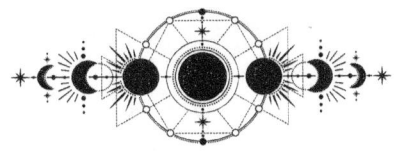

# Dreams

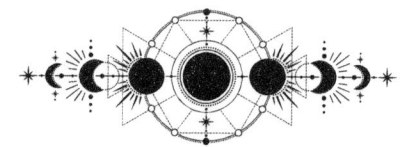

# Dreams

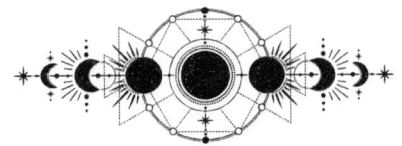

# *Dreams*

*Date:*

*How do I feel after waking?*

*What was the main theme of my dream?*

*Setting of dream ...*

*Symbols, metaphors, people, animals and their possible meaning ...*

*How does the dream relate to my life?*

*Reflection*

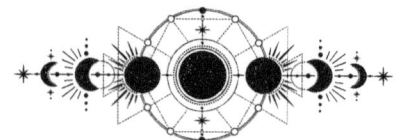

# Dreams

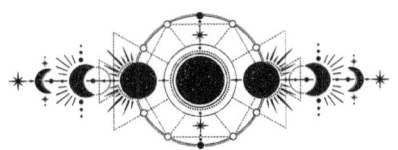

# Dreams

_____
_____
_____
_____
_____
_____
_____
_____
_____
_____
_____
_____
_____
_____
_____
_____
_____
_____
_____
_____
_____
_____
_____

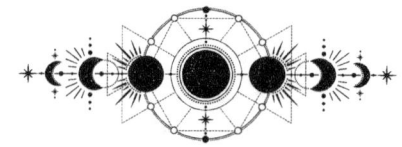

# *Dreams*

_____
_____
_____
_____
_____
_____
_____
_____
_____
_____
_____
_____
_____
_____
_____
_____
_____
_____
_____
_____
_____
_____
_____
_____

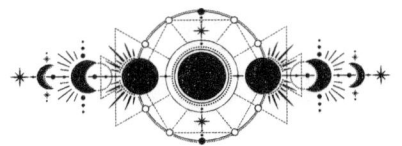

# *Dreams*

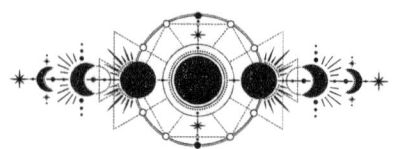

# Dreams

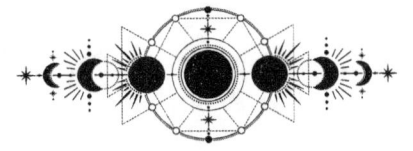

# Dreams

Date:

### How do I feel after waking?

### What was the main theme of my dream?

### Setting of dream ...

### Symbols, metaphors, people, animals and their possible meaning ...

### How does the dream relate to my life?

### Reflection

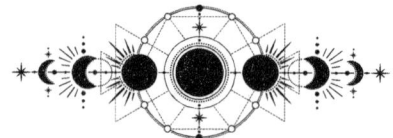

# *Dreams*

_____
_____
_____
_____
_____
_____
_____
_____
_____
_____
_____
_____
_____
_____
_____
_____
_____
_____
_____
_____
_____
_____

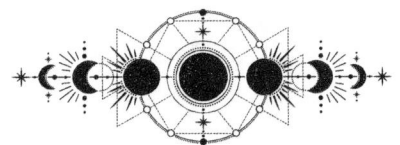

# Dreams

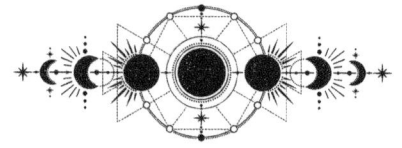

# Dreams

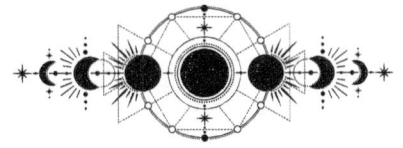

# Dreams

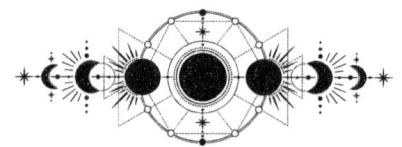

# Dreams

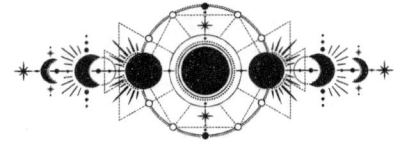

# Dreams

Date:

### How do I feel after waking?

### What was the main theme of my dream?

### Setting of dream ...

### Symbols, metaphors, people, animals and their possible meaning ...

### How does the dream relate to my life?

### Reflection

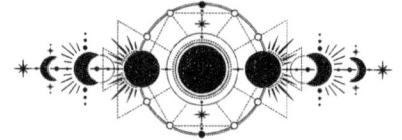

# *Dreams*

_____
_____
_____
_____
_____
_____
_____
_____
_____
_____
_____
_____
_____
_____
_____
_____
_____
_____
_____
_____
_____
_____
_____
_____

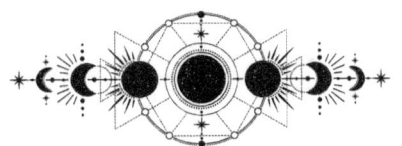

# Dreams

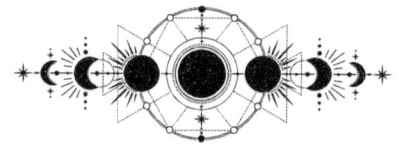

# *Dreams*

_____
_____
_____
_____
_____
_____
_____
_____
_____
_____
_____
_____
_____
_____
_____
_____
_____
_____
_____
_____
_____

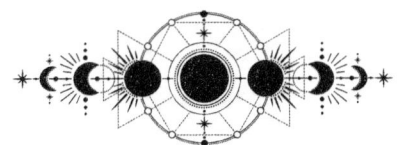

# *Dreams*

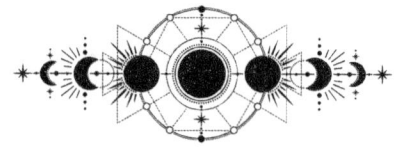

# Dreams

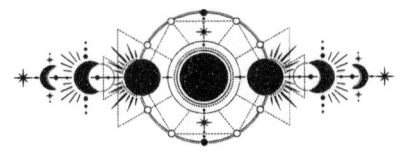

# Dreams

Date:

### How do I feel after waking?

### What was the main theme of my dream?

### Setting of dream ...

### Symbols, metaphors, people, animals and their possible meaning ...

### How does the dream relate to my life?

### Reflection

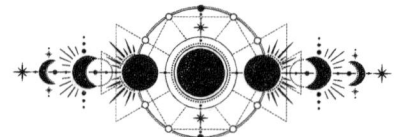

# Dreams

_____
_____
_____
_____
_____
_____
_____
_____
_____
_____
_____
_____
_____
_____
_____
_____
_____
_____
_____
_____
_____
_____

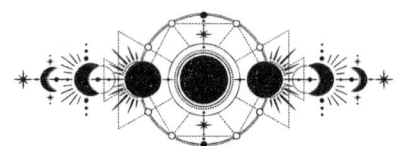

# Dreams

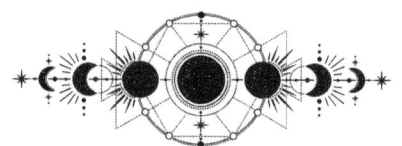

# Dreams

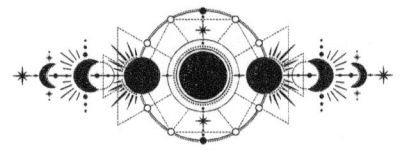

# Dreams

_____
_____
_____
_____
_____
_____
_____
_____
_____
_____
_____
_____
_____
_____
_____
_____
_____
_____
_____
_____
_____
_____
_____

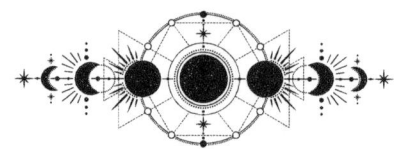

# Dreams

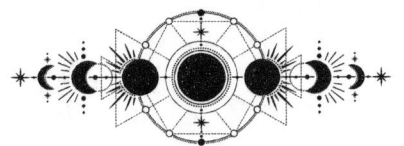

# *Dreams*

Date:

*How do I feel after waking?*

*What was the main theme of my dream?*

*Setting of dream ...*

*Symbols, metaphors, people, animals and their possible meaning ...*

*How does the dream relate to my life?*

*Reflection*

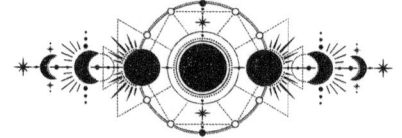

# *Dreams*

_____
_____
_____
_____
_____
_____
_____
_____
_____
_____
_____
_____
_____
_____
_____
_____
_____
_____
_____
_____
_____

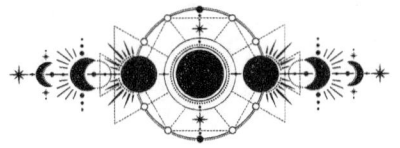

# Dreams

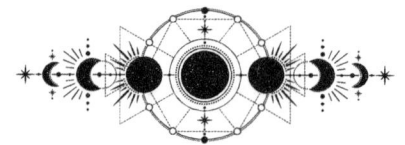

# *Dreams*

_____
_____
_____
_____
_____
_____
_____
_____
_____
_____
_____
_____
_____
_____
_____
_____
_____
_____
_____
_____

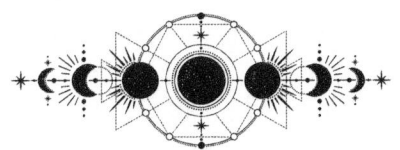

# Dreams

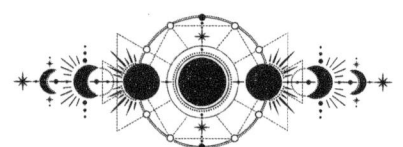

# Dreams

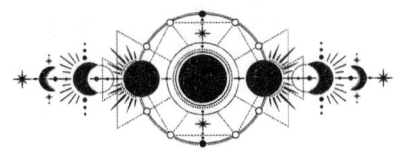

# *Dreams*

Date:

*How do I feel after waking?*

*What was the main theme of my dream?*

*Setting of dream ...*

*Symbols, metaphors, people, animals and their possible meaning ...*

*How does the dream relate to my life?*

*Reflection*

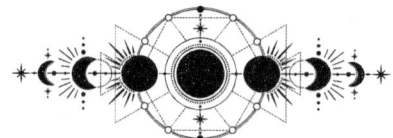

# Dreams

_____
_____
_____
_____
_____
_____
_____
_____
_____
_____
_____
_____
_____
_____
_____
_____
_____
_____
_____
_____
_____
_____
_____

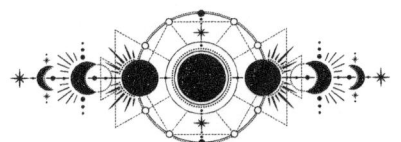

# Dreams

_____
_____
_____
_____
_____
_____
_____
_____
_____
_____
_____
_____
_____
_____
_____
_____
_____
_____
_____
_____
_____
_____
_____

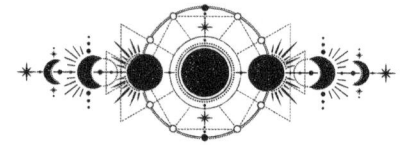

# Dreams

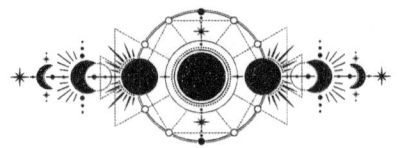

# Dreams

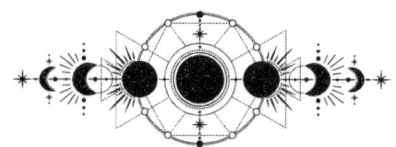

# Dreams

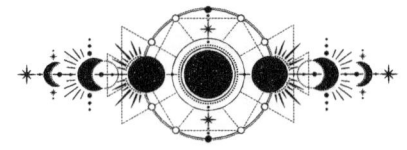

# Dreams

Date:

How do I feel after waking?

What was the main theme of my dream?

Setting of dream ...

Symbols, metaphors, people, animals and their possible meaning ...

How does the dream relate to my life?

Reflection

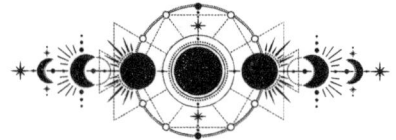

# *Dreams*

_____
_____
_____
_____
_____
_____
_____
_____
_____
_____
_____
_____
_____
_____
_____
_____
_____
_____
_____
_____
_____
_____

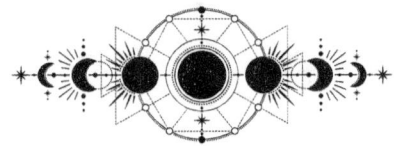

# Dreams

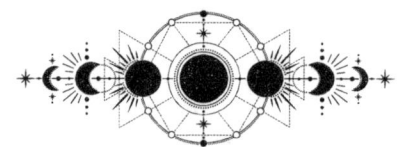

# *Dreams*

_____
_____
_____
_____
_____
_____
_____
_____
_____
_____
_____
_____
_____
_____
_____
_____
_____
_____
_____
_____
_____
_____

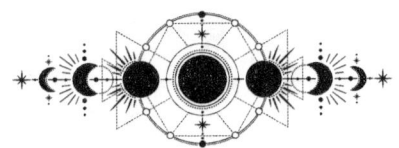

# Dreams

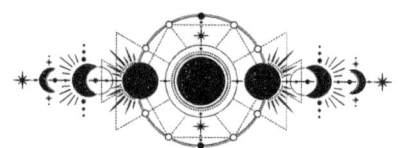

# Dreams

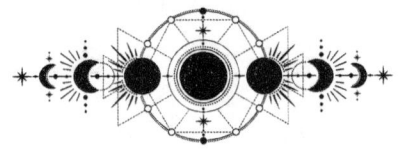

# Dreams

Date:

### How do I feel after waking?

### What was the main theme of my dream?

### Setting of dream ...

### Symbols, metaphors, people, animals and their possible meaning ...

### How does the dream relate to my life?

### Reflection

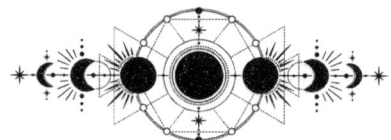

# *Dreams*

_____
_____
_____
_____
_____
_____
_____
_____
_____
_____
_____
_____
_____
_____
_____
_____
_____
_____
_____
_____
_____
_____

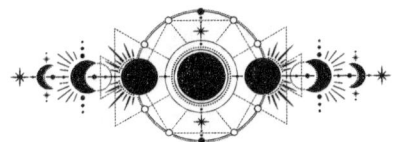

# Dreams

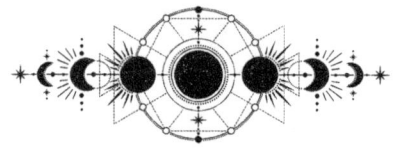

# *Dreams*

_____
_____
_____
_____
_____
_____
_____
_____
_____
_____
_____
_____
_____
_____
_____
_____
_____
_____
_____
_____
_____
_____

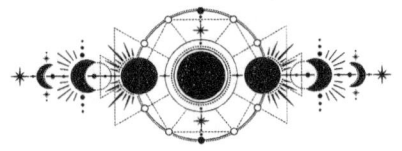

# *Dreams*

_____
_____
_____
_____
_____
_____
_____
_____
_____
_____
_____
_____
_____
_____
_____
_____
_____
_____
_____
_____
_____
_____
_____

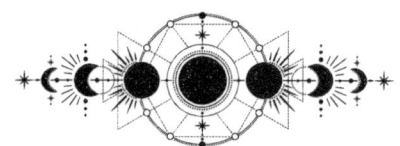

# Dreams

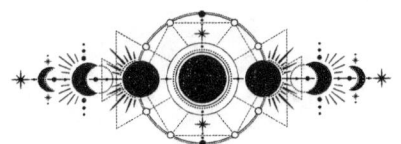

# Dreams

Date:

### How do I feel after waking?

### What was the main theme of my dream?

### Setting of dream ...

### Symbols, metaphors, people, animals and their possible meaning ...

### How does the dream relate to my life?

### Reflection

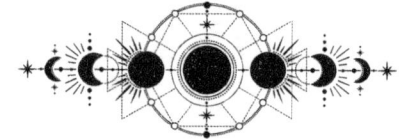

# Dreams

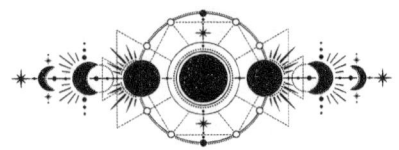

# Dreams

_____
_____
_____
_____
_____
_____
_____
_____
_____
_____
_____
_____
_____
_____
_____
_____
_____
_____
_____
_____
_____
_____

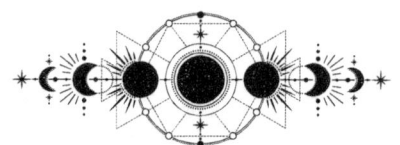

# *Dreams*

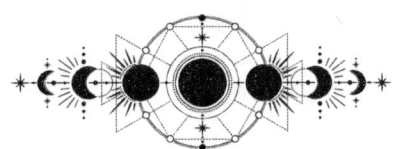

# *Dreams*

_____
_____
_____
_____
_____
_____
_____
_____
_____
_____
_____
_____
_____
_____
_____
_____
_____
_____
_____
_____
_____

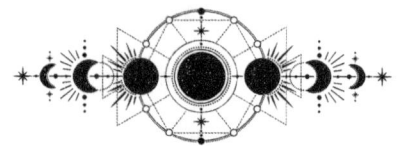

# Dreams

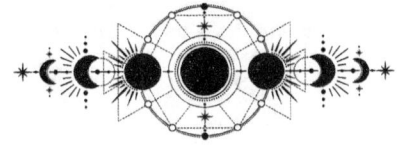

# Dreams

Date:

### How do I feel after waking?

### What was the main theme of my dream?

### Setting of dream ...

### Symbols, metaphors, people, animals and their possible meaning ...

### How does the dream relate to my life?

### Reflection

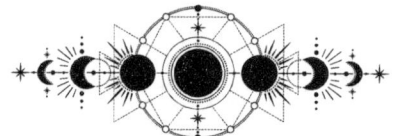

# Dreams

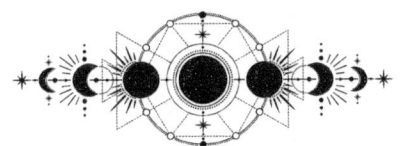

# *Dreams*

_____
_____
_____
_____
_____
_____
_____
_____
_____
_____
_____
_____
_____
_____
_____
_____
_____
_____
_____
_____
_____
_____
_____
_____
_____
_____

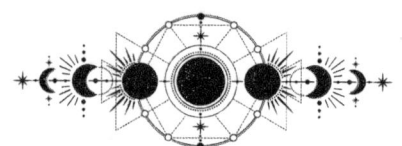

# *Dreams*

_____
_____
_____
_____
_____
_____
_____
_____
_____
_____
_____
_____
_____
_____
_____
_____
_____
_____
_____
_____
_____
_____

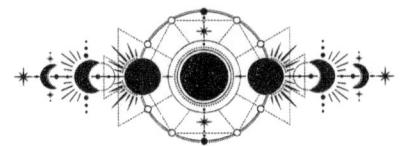

# *Dreams*

_____
_____
_____
_____
_____
_____
_____
_____
_____
_____
_____
_____
_____
_____
_____
_____
_____
_____
_____
_____
_____
_____
_____

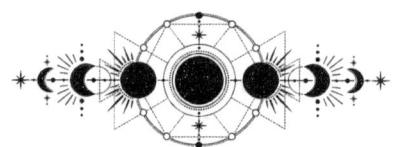

# Dreams

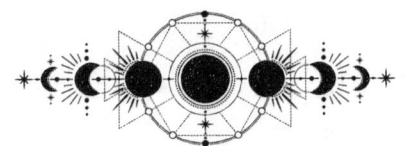

# Dreams

Date:

How do I feel after waking?

What was the main theme of my dream?

Setting of dream ...

Symbols, metaphors, people, animals and their possible meaning ...

How does the dream relate to my life?

Reflection

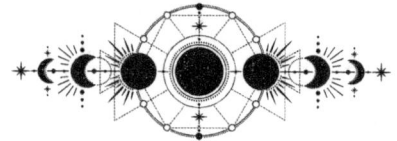

# *Dreams*

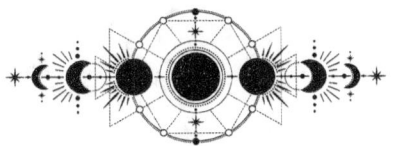

# Dreams

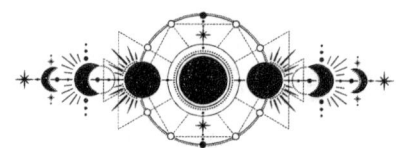

# *Dreams*

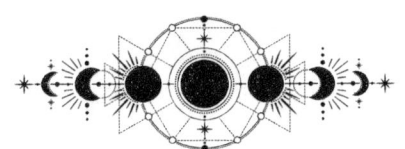

# Dreams

_____
_____
_____
_____
_____
_____
_____
_____
_____
_____
_____
_____
_____
_____
_____
_____
_____
_____
_____
_____
_____
_____
_____
_____

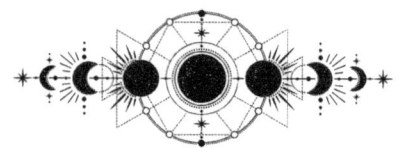

# Dreams

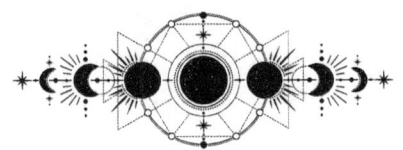

# Dreams

Date:

### How do I feel after waking?

### What was the main theme of my dream?

### Setting of dream ...

### Symbols, metaphors, people, animals and their possible meaning ...

### How does the dream relate to my life?

### Reflection

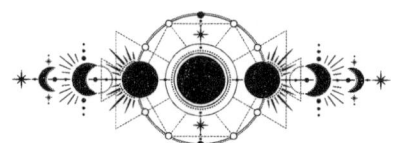

# *Dreams*

_____
_____
_____
_____
_____
_____
_____
_____
_____
_____
_____
_____
_____
_____
_____
_____
_____
_____
_____
_____
_____
_____
_____
_____

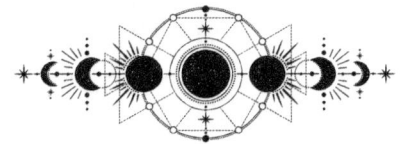

# Dreams

_____
_____
_____
_____
_____
_____
_____
_____
_____
_____
_____
_____
_____
_____
_____
_____
_____
_____
_____
_____
_____
_____

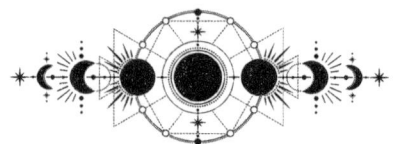

# *Dreams*

_____
_____
_____
_____
_____
_____
_____
_____
_____
_____
_____
_____
_____
_____
_____
_____
_____
_____
_____
_____
_____
_____

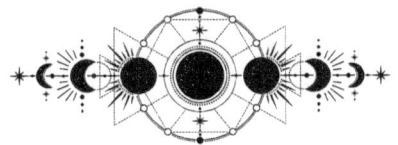

# *Dreams*

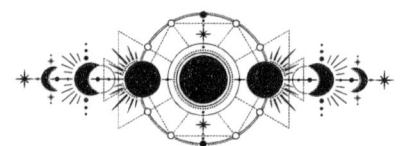

# Dreams

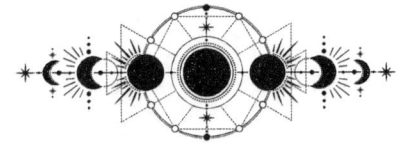

# Dreams

Date:

### How do I feel after waking?

### What was the main theme of my dream?

### Setting of dream ...

### Symbols, metaphors, people, animals and their possible meaning ...

### How does the dream relate to my life?

### Reflection

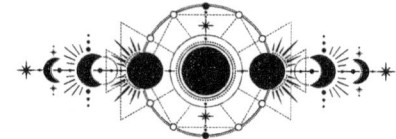

# *Dreams*

_____
_____
_____
_____
_____
_____
_____
_____
_____
_____
_____
_____
_____
_____
_____
_____
_____
_____
_____
_____
_____

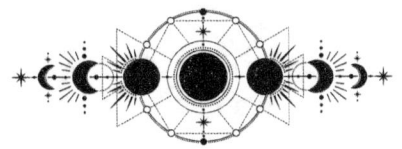

# Dreams

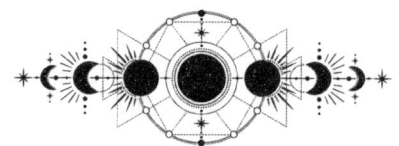

# Dreams

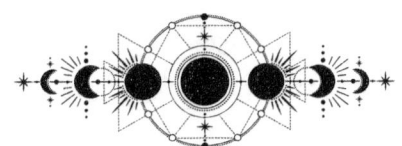

# *Dreams*

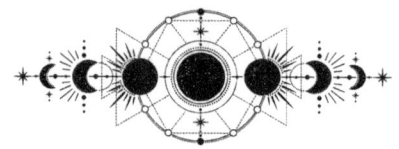

# Dreams

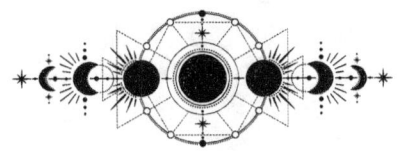

# *Dreams*

Date:

*How do I feel after waking?*

*What was the main theme of my dream?*

*Setting of dream ...*

*Symbols, metaphors, people, animals and their possible meaning ...*

*How does the dream relate to my life?*

*Reflection*

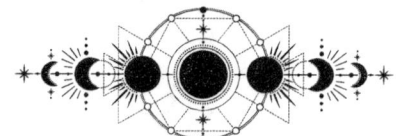

# Dreams

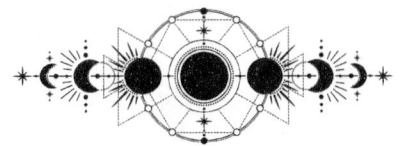

# *Dreams*

_____
_____
_____
_____
_____
_____
_____
_____
_____
_____
_____
_____
_____
_____
_____
_____
_____
_____
_____
_____
_____
_____
_____

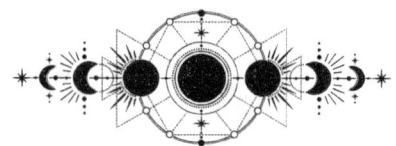

# *Dreams*

_____
_____
_____
_____
_____
_____
_____
_____
_____
_____
_____
_____
_____
_____
_____
_____
_____
_____
_____
_____
_____
_____
_____

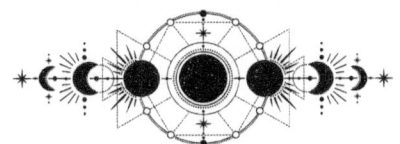

# *Dreams*

_____
_____
_____
_____
_____
_____
_____
_____
_____
_____
_____
_____
_____
_____
_____
_____
_____
_____
_____
_____
_____
_____
_____
_____

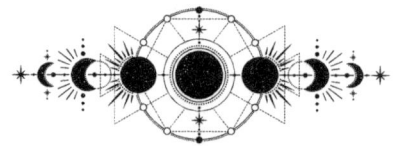

# Dreams

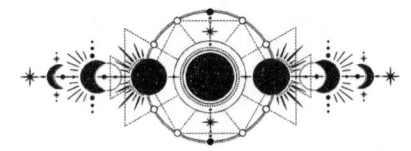

# Dreams

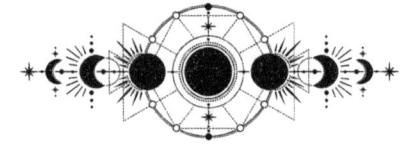

# Dreams

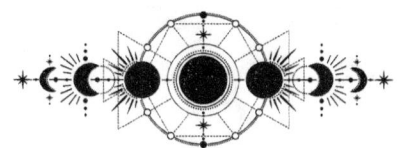

# Dreams

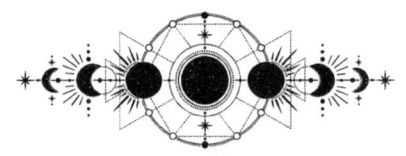

www.ingramcontent.com/pod-product-compliance
Lightning Source LLC
Chambersburg PA
CBHW080346300426
44110CB00019B/2522